HOW TO MEND A KEA

+ OTHER FABULOUS FIX-IT TALES FROM WILDBASE HOSPITAL

JANET HUNT

MASSEY UNIVERSITY PRESS

WHAT'S IN THIS BOOK

HOW TO READ THIS BOOK

This book is in three sections. Part 1, 'Hello there, Wildbase', is a small introduction to the wildlife hospital and the people who work in it as well as to the wider conservation community.

Part 2, 'How to mend a kea', follows one animal's Wildbase story. Each patient is different, from the tiniest frog to the largest seabird, and even though there are so many things to go wrong — accidents, breakages, illness, starvation, infection — and so many body parts to potentially be affected — heads, blood, bones, organs, bills, flippers, feathers, feet — similar processes are followed. Every day at the hospital has a basic pattern, and every case traces a similar trajectory from illness to health. We glimpse a little of these through Kea's story.

Part 3, 'Washing, cleaning, breaking, mending, stitching & feeding', adds a selection of 11 more case histories, beginning with the largest, the 2011 emergency response to the grounding of the MV *Rena*, and ending with snapshots to give some idea of the great range of patients cared for at Wildbase.

Through them, in total, you will have some idea of the extent and variety of patients and cases that pass through Wildbase. Some don't have happy endings, but the majority do: the team likes to say that there's nothing better than seeing the *tail end* of their patients, as they go out the door back to their homes.

Many of the images in this book come from the Wildbase collection. Some have been taken by Dave, Massey University's photographer, using the best of gear; others have been taken with cellphones — after all, medicine, not publishing, is the aim. Some of the photos go onto the Wildbase Facebook page. Long after you have finished reading this book, you can keep up with the happenings at the hospital by checking it out. *Go, Wildbase!*

PART 1

HELLO THERE, WILDBASE

INTRODUCTIONS

MASSEY UNIVERSITY

WILDBASE

HOSPITAL

WHAT IS WILDBASE?

Wildbase is the hospital for sick and injured native animals from all over New Zealand. It is part of the Institute of Veterinary, Animal and Biomedical Sciences at Massey University in Palmerston North. It is also a training hospital for vets, wildlife technicians and nurses.

The hospital was opened in 2002. For 15 years it was located in a very small, crowded space in the veterinary school, but in early 2017 it moved to a new clinic that is 10 times larger. The rooms are clean and bright and include a surgery, an intensive care ward, holding wards named after native trees, different types and sizes of cages and a meeting room.

The hospital also now has its own vehicle (below), a wildlife ambulance sponsored by Toyota and Fly Palmy. The ambulance makes life easier when the team needs to pick up and deliver patients around town and to the airport.

The hospital building: Wildbase is on the ground floor on the left.

Two kinds of native animal come to Wildbase. ('Animal' means birds as well as creatures such as mammals and reptiles.)

1 • RARE AND ENDANGERED NATIVE ANIMALS

The New Zealand Threat Classification System ranks species that are in danger of dying out. Sometimes there are hardly any of the species left, like kākāpō or takahē. These animals come from all over the country, often by air, occasionally from as far away as Stewart Island, the subantarctic islands or the Chathams. (There's a list of New Zealand Threat Classification categories on page 62 of this book.)

2 • COMMON NATIVE ANIMALS

These are the ones we often see in our daily lives — creatures like tūī, piwakawaka (fantail), kererū, pūkeko and the harrier hawk. They come to Wildbase from Manawatū, Taranaki and Hawke's Bay, but no further.

The 'commons' are treated because they are part of the Wildbase world. They are often similar to their more rare and endangered relatives: pūkeko are like takahē, and harriers are like falcons, for instance. This means that while Wildbase is helping a local bird, the team is also learning and practising skills for working with those super-endangered, really precious creatures. The hospital also cares for a few other non-native birds and the occasional pet reptile.

It's a mix: rare and endangered native species are side-by-side with common native species.

[1] Kererū (common); [2] Otago skink (rare/endangered); [3] morepork (common); [4] kiwi (rare/endangered); [5] Antipodes Island parakeet chick (rare/endangered); [6] green turtle (rare/endangered).

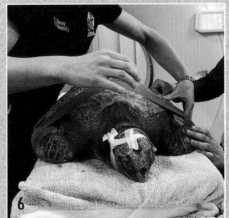

MEET THE TEAM

At Wildbase there are always at least two people working with the animals.

★ **DUTY VET** Four vets work on a roster so there is always at least one at the clinic.

★ **WILDLIFE TECHNICIANS** There are three, who also work on a roster.

★ **TRAINEES** Most times there are student vets, technicians and nurses present in the hospital, getting useful experience, watching and learning, helping out, preparing food, feeding the animals, giving medication and cleaning up.

The Wildbase team in the operating theatre on the day of the opening of the new hospital, 27 January 2017.

BRETT
Veterinarian
Wildbase Director

REBECCA
Veterinarian

CARINA
Technician

JESSICA
Veterinarian

PAULINE
Senior technician

MEGAN
Veterinarian

CHRISTINE
Technician

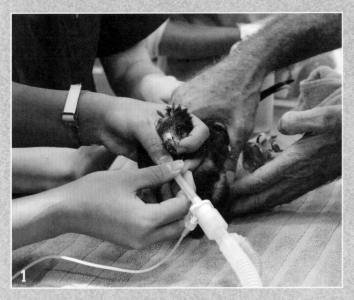

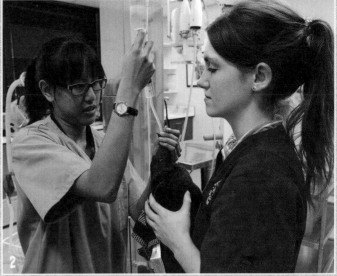

TALK TO ME

Just as in a sports team, everyone has a part to play and it's critical that they share information and help one another. There must be no mix-ups, especially when there are several of the same species in the hospital at the same time.

★ **WHITEBOARDS** These are dotted around the clinic. They tell the team:
  • which animal is in, what's wrong with it and where it is (which cage, in which ward)
  • what's happening each day
  • what's on the menu for each animal (the whiteboard in the kitchen)

★ **PAPER NOTES** Handwritten records on a clipboard follow each patient. They record details such as why it's in hospital, what treatment it's receiving, and what it eats. Each animal has a unique number.

★ **COMPUTER** Handwritten notes are transferred to the computer every day along with information such as X-rays.

★ **MEETINGS** There's a weekly team get-together to discuss what's happening with patients. There are also daily talks and conversations to share information and to continue to improve the skills of the team.

1 Helping hands: a harrier hawk with a fractured wing being anaesthetised.

2 Trainee vets Jasmine and Eva work together to 'crop tube' a kererū. The tube delivers food or liquid down the bird's throat directly into the first part of its digestive system (the crop).

PATIENT RECORD + MEDS

MENU

Room	Species/Name	Diet	Presentation	Nº
	Kereru	100g mix BID		1
	Whio	Kereru mix, teal pellets, bloodworms		1
	Harrier	1 chk c/u		1
	Kiwi Hakurangi	50g am 200g pm		1
	A.I. Parakeet	Parrot seed + Kereru mix		1
	Teal	pellets + Kereru mix BID		1
	Kea/Kaka	nectar, variety of fruits/veg/seed/pellets		2
PP	'Cadbury' Galah (PP)	seed/pellets + fruit + veg, 10ml Recovery am		1
				1

DAILY PLANNER

Monday

8-9 TX - Cadbury bandage - order drugs.

9-10 - Antipodes - Whio.

10 - Toffee Discharge (PAH) + 2x loakan ki boxes.

10-80 Tma bandaged

11:00 Morgan - Tortise consult.

1pm, Paukarangi - Beak Rads.

Techs
Send Toxity + heartworm to Nnt Lab.
Order emersion oil

Soon 022 0762421

DIGITAL RECORD

WORK WITH ME

Does the thought of helping endangered creatures inspire you? Would you like to work in a place like Wildbase?

There are many options open to you, but be warned! The numbers of jobs in this field are limited and lots of people want them. You're going to have to be the best!

★ **WILDLIFE VETERINARIAN** You could first train at Massey for a degree in veterinary science, and then specialise in caring for wildlife. It takes five years to become a vet.

★ **WILDLIFE TECHNICIANS** You could train at Massey for a degree in veterinary technology, and then specialise in caring for wildlife. It takes three years to become a vet tech.

For either of these positions, you need to be a whizz at science, be patient and good with animals *and* with people, be observant, organised, a fantastic communicator, and physically fit and strong. Working with animals is challenging and can be hard — but don't let that put you off. It can also be immensely satisfying.

The good news is that even if you don't end up working at Wildbase, your skills will be welcome in many other places, including the Department of Conservation and New Zealand's many wildlife sanctuaries.

Eva Laing is a recently qualified vet from Scotland who spent some time helping out and observing at Wildbase after she had finished her training. Brett Gartrell, the Wildbase director, is showing her around one of the Antipodes Island parakeets.

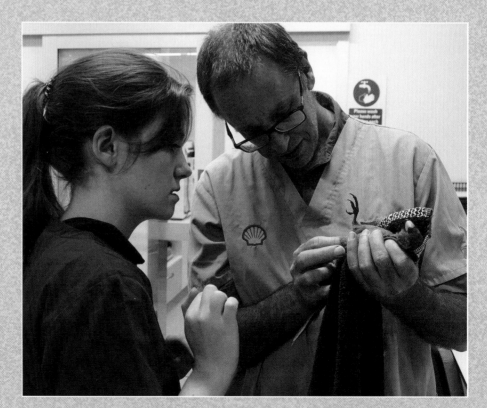

COMINGS & GOINGS

Sick and injured creatures are sent to Wildbase by:

★ **THE GENERAL PUBLIC** Individuals, schools and organisations such as Forest & Bird who come across hurt wildlife.

★ **VET CLINICS & THE DEPARTMENT OF CONSERVATION (DOC)** Vet clinics and DOC are the first places most people go when they have wild animals in distress. Sometimes DOC people pass hurt animals to the vet. *Everyone links up with everyone else. It's a huge network.*

★ **BIRD RESCUE CENTRES** Sometimes they look after wild creatures themselves with the help of the local vet. And sometimes they send patients on to Wildbase.

★ **WILDLIFE PARKS & SANCTUARIES** Some are on this country's many offshore islands, like Kāpiti, Tiritiri Matangi or Hauturu, while a growing number are mainland islands such as Zealandia; some are open to the public, others are off-limits. All of them care for and breed rare and endangered New Zealand wildlife and need to call on Wildbase at times.

Who, me? A morepork with a damaged bill at Bird Rescue, Turakina.

When a patient is well enough to leave Wildbase, but not quite ready to be released in the wild, it will go back to the people who sent it to the hospital, as long as they have facilities and are able to care for it.

If not, it might go to a halfway house, a dedicated recovery and rehabilitation centre, such as . . .

BIRD RESCUE AT TURAKINA

The Whanganui-Manawatū Bird Rescue Centre at Turakina has cared for birds for over 30 years. It's run by volunteers and funded by op-shop sales and by donations. It does a great job, working with Wildbase to help over 1000 birds a year.

Aviaries and pens of all shapes, materials and sizes are dotted around a grassy, reedy paddock. They contain birds such as kiwi, kererū, morepork, tūī and harrier hawks, all in varying stages of repair. And a talkative magpie!

The manager, Dawne Morton, has dedicated her life to the birds. She knows the history of each one and is expert at judging when they are ready to be returned to the places they came from.

WITH MASSEY UNIVERSITY
AND PALMERSTON NORTH
CITY COUNCIL

The harrier enclosure at Bird Rescue, Turakina. Circular aviaries are a good way to exercise these jittery high fliers without giving them so much space they get up speed and crash.

THE CENTRAL ENERGY TRUST WILDBASE RECOVERY CENTRE

It doesn't exist yet, but plans and fundraising are under way for a national wildlife recovery centre that will replace the aviaries on the Esplanade in Palmerston North with a specially designed, world-class rehabilitation centre.

The new facility will be owned by Palmerston North City Council and operated in partnership with Massey University.

Like the Bird Rescue Centre in Turakina, the recovery centre will take patients when they are ready to leave the hospital and give them time to gain weight and fully recover strength before they are released.

Because it's so close to the hospital, animals and staff will be able to move easily between the two.

The recovery centre will also be a major visitor attraction, a place where the public can view recovering patients without disturbing them, as well as being a destination with special programmes for school groups.

The first sod was turned in April 2017 and all going well, the centre will be up and running by 2018.

PART 2

HOW TO MEND A KEA

PATIENT #78129, WILDBASE 2017

This image, taken on a cellphone shortly after Kea's arrival at Wildbase, is the only one of him as he was at that time. He is propped on his right leg, supporting himself with his badly out-of-kilter left leg high up the wall.

Kea is broken, that's for sure. He is first spotted in September 2016 by a worker at the Meridian Power Station at West Arm, on Lake Manapouri. His left leg sticks out like a street sign, pointing nowhere. It's useless. He's hopping on his right leg, which is infected and swollen and is doing all the work. He's thin. His feathers are scruffy.

The worker tries many times to catch him, but despite his handicap, Kea escapes. He's young, he's tough and he's smart. He's living rough, surviving by rummaging for scraps near the visitor centre and the workers' accommodation.

He is finally caught on 30 December. Charlie, who works at the hostel, comes out of the shower block. She's wearing shorts, t-shirt and sandals and has a towel wrapped around her hair. Kea is hanging about in the bushes, watching. She wiggles her toes at him.

Kea is fascinated and sidles closer for a look. The toes look like huhu grubs! What do they taste like?

Aaarkk!

She grabs him. She throws the towel over Kea's head and his fossicking days are over — for now, at least.

THE LONG FLIGHT NORTH

Kea wriggles and struggles, kicks and bites, but in no time at all he's in a bin on a boat crossing Lake Manapouri. He's taken to the DOC office in Te Anau. DOC ranger Max Smart calls local wildlife lover and vet Nigel Dougherty: Can this bird be saved or should it be humanely killed? What is wrong with it anyway?

Darn it, they decide. It's worth a shot. Why not send him to Wildbase?

There's no time to lose. Still in his container, Kea is driven to Queenstown, two hours away.

Kea live in the forests and the high country. They rule the skies and regularly fly over the tops of mountains, but this time, Kea soars higher and farther than ever before, in the cargo hold of an Air New Zealand jet, bound for Palmerston North. Two flights later he's unloaded into the Wildbase ambulance and is on his way to the hospital. It's New Year's Eve. It's going to be four long months before he sees the outside world again.

CASE # 78129

KEA / MOUNTAIN PARROT
Nestor notabilis

Conservation status: Nationally endangered.

Admitted: 31/12/2016

Injury: Leg dislocation/fracture.

Kea are the world's only alpine parrots. There's a population of up to 7000, although it's not possible to be precise — they are difficult to count because wild kea live in the forests and above the treeline, high in the mountains.

Kea's feathers are perfect camouflage for their rocky, mossy world.

YOUR TICKET, PLEASE?
Kea flies for free. Air New Zealand and the Department of Conservation have a special deal to transport sick and injured endangered animals to and from Wildbase at no cost.

The treatment of every creature admitted to Wildbase follows a similar pattern. It's much the same as for a person going to hospital, but with one important difference: *wild creatures can't tell you what happened to them.* Sometimes the humans who bring them in tell the team what they know about the animal's history, but mostly the Wildbase vets and techs must be detectives as well as doctors.

DAY 1: A FIRST ONCE-OVER

A record is created for Kea as soon as he enters the building. He's given a number (#78129) and is tracked digitally as well as with handwritten notes on a clipboard. Everything about his treatment is documented: what he eats, his medication and how he is going.

The Wildbase team tries very hard not to tame patients. It's not good for the birds to rely on people because sooner or later they will be free, living healthy independent lives in the wild. They are not humans and that's why they (mostly) don't have names.

Instead, patients are identified by species, by where they come from and sometimes, especially if they have been bred in captivity, by their microchip.

Kea is simply: 'Kea, Patient #78129'.

1 • ONTO THE SCALES FOR KEA

It's vital that every animal is weighed every day. It is wrapped in a towel to keep it still, placed on scales and a reading is taken. Then the weight of the towel is subtracted.

If it is gaining weight, that's good: it means the patient is coping with being in hospital and getting better. If it is losing weight, that's a cause for concern.

When he came in, Kea weighed 747 grams. A full-grown, healthy male kea will weigh between 900 and 1100 grams, so even though he was a young bird, he had a little way to go.

ALIENS!

How strange and scary it must be for Kea coming into Wildbase. One minute he's in his familiar forest and upland world. Even though he is unwell, he comes and goes as he pleases. He can still fly. He can check out interesting things he finds. There are other kea.

Without warning he is *birdnapped* and his world is upside-down.

In the clinic everything is bright, shiny sterile and hard. The walls are white. The tables and benches and cages are gleaming stainless steel. People peer and prod at him. It must be like being abducted by aliens!

As you can see from the readout on the scales, Kea weighs in at a healthy 940.1 grams. This is near the end of his time at Wildbase. He's put on almost 200 grams.

2 • LET'S LOOK AT YOU

Jessica is the vet on duty when Kea arrives. She carefully examines him, from the top of his head and the tip of his bill, to the end of his claws. Gentle fingers ruffle his feathers, pull out his wings, press his tummy. Large eyes look into his bright eyes and peer inside his bill.

Pauline is the vet technician who helps Jessica. She holds Kea. She listens to his heart. They tip him backwards and forwards to see if his tail moves and if his spine is OK (it is).

But it's Kea's legs that are worrying: his street-sign left leg and his swollen right leg. They will get a much closer look. Tomorrow.

Kea is injected with drugs to reduce inflammation and to lower pain and prevent him from suffering.

3 • OPEN WIDE

Because they are unwell, most animals are dehydrated and starving when they come into Wildbase. They haven't had enough to drink or eat. Sometimes fluids are directly injected into a vein.

Often, because an animal is too frightened to eat and doesn't know how to eat out of a bowl anyway, its bill is opened wide, a tube is gently pushed down into the crop and liquid food is squeezed in from a syringe. This gives the animal energy for the next day.

Kea doesn't need that because he's eating by himself. He is given a bowl of fruit, veges, seeds and pellets and he tucks in and has an overnight feast.

4 • SAFE & WARM

Many new admissions are very ill. An animal might be a tough dude like Kea or it might be so weak and skinny it can hardly stand. Very often it will go into an incubator in intensive care. At 29 degrees, it's toasty in there. A bird's usual body temperature is around 40 degrees so that's just comfortable.

Kea is remarkably sturdy and doesn't need the incubator. The hospital is very small and cramped but they find a place for him.

He goes directly into a cage that's on top of a stack of three.

5 • TREATMENT TIME

That's almost it for Kea's first day.

In the later afternoon, about 3 p.m., all the creatures in Wildbase are fed and given medication — just like the rounds in a hospital. Darkness falls, the humans go home and everything is quiet.

Kea is in his cage. Is he still wondering: *What just happened? Where did those huhu grubs go?*

Zzzzz.

ARGH! IT'S TOO MUCH

Stress kills! In the wild, the stress response keeps animals alert and agile to escape danger. They *fight* if they can or *fly* if that's their best option.

But if that stress doesn't go away, it is deadly. A condition called 'capture myopathy' kills a wild animal once it has gone beyond terrified.

There is no cure. It's best to try to make sure it doesn't happen.

That's why it's important to handle the patients as little and as quickly as possible, and to keep their environment dark and quiet. Many of the Wildbase cages have plastic box hidey-houses and often there is a towel hanging over the front, just to keep things shady.

(*Shhh!* There's a kiwi in this one.)

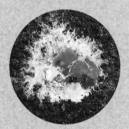
DAY 2: WORK-UP

Kea is rested and comfortable. It's time to investigate the inner bird.

1 • A MESSAGE FROM POO

When Kea is taken from his cage in the morning Pauline scoops a dropping sample into a plastic pottle like this one. Poo tells heaps about what's going on inside a patient.

1

★ **FOOD** It gives clues about what he has been eating.

★ **PARASITES** Birds (and other creatures including humans) can be hosts to a great many parasites, mainly in their stomachs. Most are worm-like (nematodes, cestoda and trematoda) but some are protozoa, so small they live inside the animal's cells. Often they are not a problem, but if the animal is unwell parasites multiply and take over, and it's all downhill after that.

The team looks at the sample under the microscope in the clinic. Sometimes they send it to the Parasitology Laboratory in the vet school at Massey for extra analysis.

Kea's droppings look OK. Apart from his legs, he's not doing too badly.

2 • WASHING THE CROP

The crop is like a pouch in the start of the bird's digestive system. The team puts fluid into Kea's crop through a tube and then pulls a small amount back out into a syringe.

Is anything missing? Is there something that shouldn't be there?
Just like reading the poo, this will signal if anything's out of kilter.

3 • G.A. TIME

Next, Kea is given a general anaesthetic (G.A.). A mask is placed over his head and bill, and isoflurane gas puts him to sleep, immobilising him so the team can carry out more tests. He's given more pain relief in case anything hurts.

★ **RADIOGRAPHS** (X-rays). Kea's wings and legs are stretched out so all his organs and bones show clearly on the radiographs. At least two are taken, one from the side and one from the back. The vet on duty can immediately see the results on a monitor in the clinic, the same as when humans go to the dentist.

BLOODS While Kea is still unconscious, blood is taken from a vein in the leg or the wing and is put on a slide under the microscope. It tells the team a whole lot more about his health.

It shows:

★ **RED AND WHITE BLOOD CELLS** If there are a lot of white blood cells the bird is stressed or has an infection and needs antibiotics.

★ **PROTEINS** Proteins can indicate if muscles are damaged or if organs such as the kidneys and/or the liver are failing.

★ **HYDRATION** If a patient hasn't had enough to drink, hydration levels will be low.

★ **ELEMENTS** There should be *none at all* but many animals have lead in their systems from the environment. They also sometimes have other metals such as cadmium or copper. Not good!

1 A pottle of poo.

2 A vial of blood from a patient.

3 Slides, ready to go under the microscope.

4 An older kea being X-rayed in 2014. This bird had been in an accident and had a bare broken bone sticking out of its leg. The fiery red feathers on the underside of the wings of kea and their kākā cousins were treasured by Māori and used in the making of kahu huruhuru (feather cloaks).

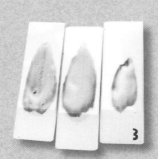

4 • MORE PHYSICAL

While Kea is still asleep it's an opportunity to take an even closer look at his body, to brush open his feathers and examine him, piece by piece.

Sometimes there are wounds or puncture marks, such as from a cat attack.

His feathers also tell a story: if new ones are growing that's a good sign, but it also means the bird needs plenty of nutritious food.

If they are tired and tatty it might just mean the bird is moulting, but it might also be another indicator of the bird's poor health — more nutritious food is needed.

When the team is finished, the isoflurane is switched off and in no time at all Kea is awake and back in his cage.

Aarrk!

What now?

Let me outta here!

DAY 3: A PLAN

Now the team knows enough to work out how to treat him. Kea has had his wonky leg for a long time and probably damaged it as a youngster in the nest. He will need surgery to break and set it in the correct place, and his other leg must also be treated. Once his legs heal, he has to learn to walk properly and get fit and able to look after himself in the wild.

Kea is admitted during the Christmas holiday and is not operated on for a week. In the meantime, he's bored and rips into things in his cage. On 3 January he tears his towel and fluffy bedding. On 5 January he works out how to undo the cage latch. He escapes but doesn't get far. He's put into a bigger cage with leafy branches to climb. His food is hidden in boxes so he has puzzles to solve.

On Tuesday 10 January, Kea goes under the scalpel.

★ **G.A.** First he is knocked out. He is lying on a Bair Hugger, a soft puffy blanket that keeps him warm.

★ **CATHETER** Next, a catheter is inserted into a vein in his right leg. A catheter is a thin tube that allows the team to give him drugs or fluids as quickly and as easily as possible.

★ **PLUCKING** All the feathers on Kea's left leg are plucked. It's wiped with sterile solutions. He's ready.

★ **OOOH!** What an intricate operation. Brett is the surgeon. He saws, cuts, pins and stitches. At the end, Kea's leg is straightened and tied into an external framework while it heals. Everything is protected by a soft bandage.

There are no photographs of Kea's surgery but it would have looked very much like this 2014 operation on a different kea.

This is the kea after the operation. The purple bandage holds the catheter in place on its other leg.

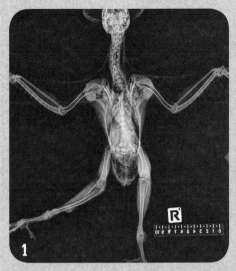
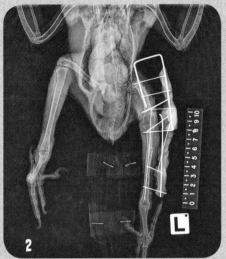

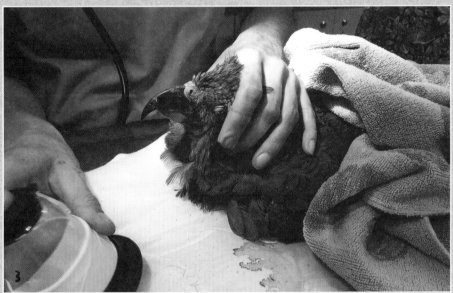

1 Kea's X-rays before his op on 10 January 2017. He looks like an angel with that halo (really, it's the oxygen mask) but *yikes! Look at the angle of that left leg.*

2 After surgery. The bone was cut and the leg was rotated and stabilised using pins and Selley's Knead-it to form an external framework to hold the pins in place. It is bandaged from the hock (ankle) to just above the stifle (knee).

3 Another kea after its operation. He's groggy and recovering from anaesthetic.

4 Kea #78129 with Wildbase director Brett, on 27 January 2017, the day the new hospital opened.

DAY 4 & ONWARD: POST-OP

The long haul begins. Slowly, slowly, over three months, Kea's wonky left leg and his infected right leg heal.

It's not easy and Kea doesn't help. He has to be stopped from chewing his feet.

More bandages. For a while it seems he has no feeling in his toes. He sits on his hocks (ankles) not his feet.

He destroys things.

He catches his toes in his towel. He has another infection that is successfully treated with mānuka honey.

Slowly, slowly. Kea recovers. Mending his legs called for top-level medical and surgical skill, but that's just the beginning.

Kea is so smart that despite Pauline's and everyone else's efforts to amuse him he's constantly bored. A human physio is consulted for ideas that will also rebuild his muscles, but the physio was not able to help.

Squats? *No . . .*

Logs and branches in one of the rooms give him climbing exercise in the day and he sleeps in his cage at night.

In February, Wildbase moves into the new hospital, and Kea now has a larger room to work out in, with branches to climb and toys that appeal to a parrot. It's a kea gymnasium!

But he does his best to destroy the room, pulling up floor coverings and eating his water bowl. It looks like vandalism but really, he is just an extraordinarily curious creature; it's all in the interests of kea science.

By March Kea is perching and hopping, using his beak as a prop.

At the end of the month he moves to the even larger display ward at the front of the clinic, where humans can look in to see recovering animals.

The team builds climbing frames from plumbers' pipes and wraps them in bright blue and green bandages so the pipes are not too slippery for Kea to scramble up and down. They scour the bush in the gullies around the campus for bigger branches.

After a few days he begins to chew Wildbase's brand-new window frames . . . so it is back to the cage for Kea.

The staff love him, but he is trying their patience. They are beginning to look forward to this kid's graduation day!

Kea's day room in the new hospital, complete with branches to climb and things to chew. Whenever anyone looks through the window he plays peekaboo, dodging from one side of the branches to the other. *Are they still watching? Yes!*

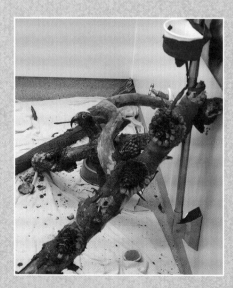

FROM THAT, TO THIS

Kea's inquisitive, often destructive, habits can be a real pain.

Can you imagine? These birds were once hunted for a bounty because people thought they attacked sheep. Between 1860 and 1970, over 150,000 kea were shot.

Killing kea was outlawed in 1986 and they are now fully protected.

Today threats to kea are from predators such as cats, dogs, weasels, stoats, ferrets, rats and possums, from lack of good food and from getting into trouble in human environments where there are rubbish dumps, roads and toxic substances such as lead (see page 48).

Please don't encourage kea to become tame. Especially, don't feed them, no matter how cute they are or how much they beg!

1 In April, towards the end of Kea's stay, Pauline and Carina make a bigger, better construction of branches and climbing pipes in the display room at the front of the clinic.

2 In the display room Kea has his first glimpse of blue skies in months. He dreams of freedom and plots an escape.

3 Kea poses while Pauline films him on her cellphone for the Wildbase Facebook page (*check it out*).

FOUR MONTHS LATER: NOW WHAT?

Kea has been at Wildbase a long time. His left leg is still a bit crooked and wobbly, but it is not sticking out any more. He tends to hop rather than walk and he favours his right leg but he's way better.

His eyes are bright, his feathers are growing.

It's time for him to go.

It's 12 April and Kea #78129 is on his way. He's been given a final check-up and is boxed up for departure at 6.35 a.m.

Off he goes, on a rewind of his journey north.

There are two flights with Air New Zealand, to Christchurch and then Queenstown, a car ride to Te Anau and a trip on the ferry *Mararoa* across the clear waters of Lake Manapouri. The boat docks at West Arm.

A short walk up the jetty.

And then . . .

Freedom.

A bill full of moss.

What was all the fuss about?

1 What is in this box? It's marked 'fragile' and addressed to the Department of Conservation.

2 Arriving at West Arm on the catamaran the *Mararoa*. Kea is being carried by DOC ranger Erina Loe, with vet Nigel Dougherty close behind.

3, 4 & OVER THE PAGE
Bruce Sutherland from Meridian Energy opens the box. *Off you go, Kea!*

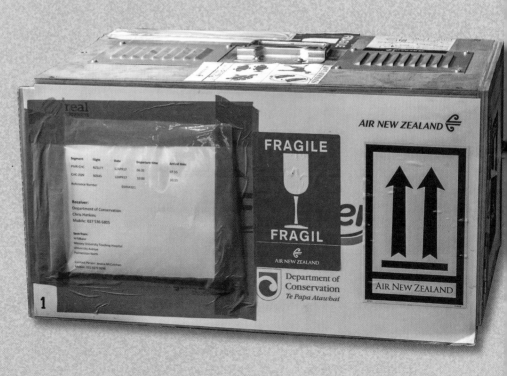

PART 3

WASHING, CLEANING, BREAKING, MENDING, STITCHING & FEEDING

WILDBASE CASE HISTORIES

[IN NO PARTICULAR ORDER]

HOW TO DE-OIL A SEABIRD

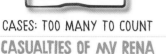

The Wildbase Oiled Wildlife Emergency Response Unit is New Zealand's No. 1 team to call when there's a wildlife crisis in New Zealand, anywhere, at any time. The unit's first big test came near the end of 2011. It was a case history to end all case histories with multiple patients, many of them little blue penguins.

In the dead of night, at 2.20 a.m. on Wednesday 5 October, a massive container ship, the MV *Rena*, struck the ridge of jagged rock near Tauranga known as the Astrolabe Reef. The boat was 236 metres long and carried 1386 containers as well as 1700 tonnes of fuel oil and 200 tonnes of marine diesel.

It was New Zealand's largest wildlife disaster. Over 350 tonnes of oil spilled out of the ship and floated on the ocean in tarry blobs. It sloshed back and forth on the waves and tides. It washed onto beaches and rocks on the small Motiti Island and on the mainland. It stuck to everything it touched. Sea-going birds such as little blue penguins, petrels, shearwaters, gannets and terns as well as coastal birds like dotterels were in great danger. They drowned when the oil destroyed the waterproofing on their feathers and they could not stay afloat.

They had little chance. Within days, dead and dying oil-smothered bodies began to wash ashore. Most were beyond help.

1 The MV *Rena* on the reef three months later. The ship broke in half on 8 January 2012 after being battered by 6-metre waves. By then many of the containers had washed overboard, but luckily, most of the fuel oil had been removed.

2, 3 & 4 The oil washed ashore with the tide: a sticky, tarry mess. It carried the blackened bodies of drowned seabirds such as this albatross and the petrels to the left.

The OWF (Oiled Wildlife Facility). Imagine organising and coordinating all the equipment, buildings and supplies as well as the people who worked in them — there were 150 Massey staff at the peak of the crisis, as well as countless volunteers.

There were 22 tents. For the wildlife there was an intake tent [1], tents for the oiled bird hospital [2], washing and rinsing tents [3], a tent for the clean bird hospital, a food storage and preparation tent and a post-mortem and body-storage tent (with refrigerators and freezers).

There were also tents for humans — a builders' tent, a meeting tent [4], a mess/kitchen/debriefing tent [5], an administration tent and tents for communications and logistics. There were also toilets.

There were oil-receiving sumps [6], five cargo containers, eight pools [7], rehabilitation aviaries [8], and crates to hold animals and to store stuff.

Duckboards had to be put down for people to walk on because with so much happening, the ground quickly became muddy and slippery.

1 Kate Wilkinson, then Minister for Conservation, visits the drying tent.
2 Puréed fish for the seabirds.
3 One of the containers.

Wildbase took charge. They established an emergency centre in the grounds of Te Maunga Wastewater Treatment Plant where there was space and buildings, plenty of water and ways to get rid of it. It was also near the badly affected beaches at Mount Maunganui and Papamoa.

The unit set up tents, holding pens, a wash-room, rehab rooms, pools and aviaries. There was a briefing tent, where everyone met each morning to plan the day ahead. There was an intake tent, where birds came first for diagnosis and a further three oil tents for them to go to. There was a fourth oil tent for seals. Plastic crates were used to hold the birds and the seals.

There was a wash-room, with bays for washing birds with specially warmed and softened water. There was a mess tent, important for Wildbase workers and the hundreds of volunteers to have somewhere to eat and take a break. There was an office.

Volunteers washed crates and prepared food for the birds by breaking up frozen fish. Builders and plumbers built and re-built cages and enclosures to meet the changing needs of each day.

And the vets, technicians, nurses, students and everyone else from Wildbase in Palmerston North dropped everything to get there, rolled up their sleeves and tackled the massive task of washing, rinsing, medicating and feeding the birds.

Thousands of birds were drowned by the oil spill. There were 2300 *known* deaths but countless others, maybe as many as 20,000, unseen at sea.

That's terrible but believe it or not, it could have been worse.

Anxious that rare New Zealand dotterels a little further down the coast would be affected if the spill increased, 60 were captured and held as an insurance population. As it turned out, the dotterels were not affected and the 60 captured birds were eventually released.

The Wildbase team learned a great deal from the event. If there is ever another disaster such as this, they will be ready.

DE-OILING A PIED SHAG

When the response team first started washing the birds, the detergent bubbled and blew all over the place as it flowed into the open receiving tank outside the tent. They were shouted at!

They covered the tank and switched to a different detergent. They found it was most effective if they wiped the bird with Canola vegetable oil first.

Washing a pied shag. The process is so stressful it can kill. It must be done as swiftly as possible.

1 A little shearwater being washed. It is very similar to a diving petrel, the birds that were among the hardest hit.

2 Drying off. The mesh prevents damage to the feet.

3 Almost ready to go.

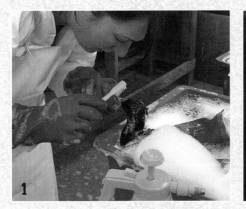

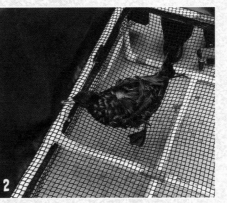

THE STORY OF A LITTLE BLUE PENGUIN (LBP)

This story is all about oil — the fuel oil from the *Rena*, the vegetable oil used to 'wash' LBP and the natural oils made by birds to keep themselves waterproof.

Little Blue Penguin was swimming and feeding near Motiti Island. She didn't see the smear of oil on the skin of the water, and in no time her thick blue-grey feathers were covered, black from flipper to foot. She only just made it to the island, where she was rescued by a wildlife patrol.

At the emergency response centre she was first lightly washed in the intake tent, especially around her eyes. Blood was taken for a TBC (total blood count) and to measure protein and glucose levels. Aside from the oil, she was in good condition but, even so, she was rested a few days until she was strong enough to be cleaned.

Then she was off to the washing tent. Washing her took from 30 to 60 minutes and was followed by rinsing and a visit to the heat lamps and blowers in the drying tent.

Then it was a matter of waiting, for the oil to be gone from the sea and for her own oily waterproofing to return. So it was into the pool for LBP, to waterproof feathers and build up muscles and swimming endurance.

She was not set free until about a month later. Some penguins were released on beaches with crowds cheering (and scaring) them on. Others, including LBP from Motiti Island, were gently dropped into the sea from a boat.

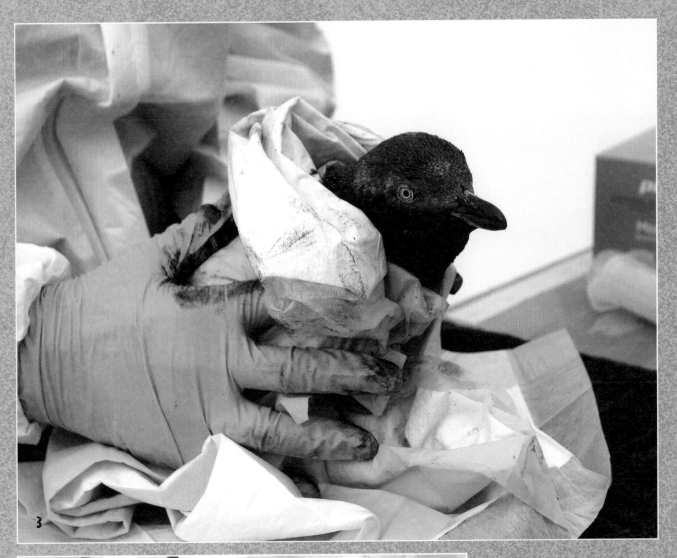

1 Making a splash in one of the pools. The rubber matting is designed to be kind to penguin feet.

2 Some penguins went through the moult while they were in captivity. When this happens, between January and March every year, they can't go to sea anyway.

3 LIttle *black* penguin.

4 Good oil versus bad! LBP is rubbed with cooking oil before being washed with detergent.

HOW TO REPAIR KIWI

CASE # 78574

NORTH ISLAND BROWN KIWI

Apteryx mantelli

Conservation status: Threatened.

Admitted: 21/01/2017

Symptom: Not eating, losing weight.

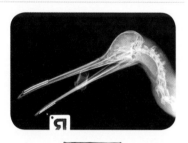

Kiwi are *weird*. They're more like mammals than birds. They have feathers like hair, whiskers like a cat, keen hearing and sharp nostrils — at the tips of their bills. They have heavy bones, near-nothing wings and no tail. They don't fly and they come out at night. Kiwi chicks are just like mini adults and are ready to go from the moment they leave the shell.

1

Kiwi is admitted on 21 January 2017. Kiwi was bred in captivity at Pukaha Mount Bruce Wildlife Centre and is just over one month old. She is one sick chick! She has no appetite and weighs only 363 grams. She falls asleep while being fed, blows bubbles in her water at night and is mostly unresponsive.

Kiwi is diagnosed with coccidiosis (intestinal parasites) and possible renal (kidney) failure. She also has hairline fractures both sides of her lower mandible (bill), which might explain the reluctance to eat. *It hurts!*

Kiwi is given fluids and antibiotics. A catheter is inserted in her leg so she can be given medication, but the bandages cause swelling and have to be removed. A tube is inserted directly through the side of Kiwi's neck into her oesophagus so she can be given liquid food.

Almost three weeks later, Kiwi's health is going in two directions at once. On the one hand, her fractured bill is getting better. On the other, she is increasingly unable to move and can only stand by using her bill as a tripod. Her parasite readings are still very high. She is given a wider range of medication.

Day by day, bit by bit, Kiwi improves. At first, she stands for a short time but gets the shakes. She is brighter. She begins to take little steps. She complains when her legs are touched. Although she is still lying down much of the time, she can stand and shuffle. She starts to eat by herself at night.

The feeding tube is removed on 16 February. Kiwi is putting on weight and weighs 418 grams. She can stand but still shuffles or does an army crawl. She's placed in a sling for up to 20 minutes at a time to keep her upright. She continues improving. By 5 March, the parasites are gone, the bill fracture is almost mended and Kiwi is well on the way to health. It is time to go back to Pukaha. She now weighs 638 grams.

Kiwi have been in New Zealand for millions of years but are in danger of disappearing from the wild. Their numbers fall every year because of habitat loss and because there are too many kiwi-killers.

Full-grown kiwi have strong legs and a mighty kick but can't defend themselves from dogs, who slaughter them *snick-snack-toss!*

Young kiwi have almost no chance. They are hurt and killed by dogs, cats, rats, stoats and ferrets. Eggs are eaten in the nest so there are no young kiwi to replace the older ones when they die.

Kee-wee! Kee-wee! Ki-wi!

1 One very small kiwi chick.

2 Kiwi using her bill as a prop. *And* sitting on her hocks.

3 Pauline places Kiwi in the incubator.

4 & 5 Another starving kiwi chick being given a general anaesthetic in a specially long face mask. Once he was unconscious he was X-rayed and given a thorough work-up to find out what was wrong.

6 An adult kiwi also has a broken bill and is crop-fed through a tube. You can see the repairs in the X-ray opposite.

7 Kiwi kai — minced meat, maybe some chopped fruit and vegetables: 50 grams in the morning and 100 grams in the afternoon.

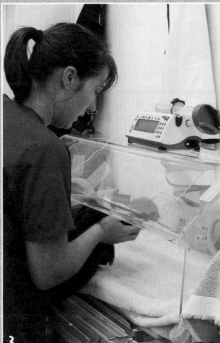

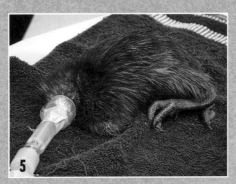

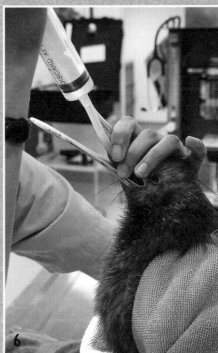

ANTIPODES ISLAND PARAKEET

Cyanoramphus unicolor

Conservation status: Naturally uncommon, which means 'at risk'.

Admitted: 26/03/17

Condition: Very, very sick.

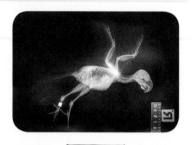

People tend to call these birds 'Antips' because their full name is a bit of a mouthful! They are New Zealand's only green-crowned parakeet.

HOW TO . . . ANTIPS

The Antipodes Island parakeet is critically ill when she comes to Wildbase. She was found on the floor of her enclosure at the Palmerston North Esplanade Aviaries, weak and breathing with difficulty.

At first, it seems she may pull through. She's examined, given fluids, pain relief and medication, and put in a darkened incubator.

But her head droops and she's not moving much.

Then, when Pauline feeds her in the afternoon the bird goes into shock. She topples sideways and it seems she is about to die. The team hold their breath and cross their fingers.

Astonishingly, she recovers and settles. *Whew.*

The next day, however, when she is being prepared for anaesthetic, it's all too much and her tiny heart stops. She is given oxygen and CPR (cardiopulmonary resuscitation) but nothing can be done. She is gone.

It's a fact of life. Every creature that lives will die sooner or later, and some animals that come to Wildbase are too unwell to be saved.

When the parakeet's body is examined by the pathology laboratory, the report is clear: her time was up, no matter what. She was 14 years old, which is old for this species of parakeet in captivity. She had aspergillosis, a fungal disease that affects birds in captivity especially when they are stressed or already ailing.

When an animal dies, the body is put in a plastic bag in the fridge and later collected by the lab for post-mortem examination. Once that is over, if it is one of the common species, the body goes to the vet school for use in veterinary training. Otherwise, the body is returned to iwi in its home area for disposal.

But where will Antip's body go? She's a long, long way from the stormy fortress of her forebears, the uninhabited, steep, rocky Antipodes Island, 860 kilometres southeast of New Zealand. There, the world's only non-captive population of Antipodes Island parakeets (3000 birds at most) has adapted to life among low plants and tussocks. They eat leaves, seeds and berries, occasionally scavenge dead birds and prey on nesting grey-backed storm petrels.

The island is a protected nature reserve. It used to be overrun by mice but in 2016 the Million Dollar Mouse project saw them off. *Excellent! More tucker for the Antips.*

1

1 Antips have such brilliant plumage! Sometimes, if a bird dies at Wildbase and is returned to iwi, the feathers are used in cloaks by qualified weavers with special permits from the Department of Conservation.

2 An adult Antipodes Island parakeet at the Esplanade Aviaries.

3 & 4 Work-up time. Going under a general anaesthetic.

5 Is the heart still beating?

6 Crop-feeding. It's tricky getting past such a curvy bill when you must work swiftly and keep stress levels down.

7 The dead Antipodes Island parakeet.

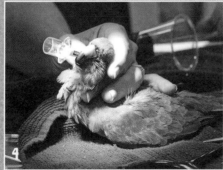

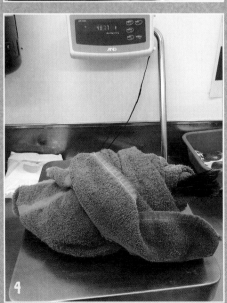

1 & 2 It's work-up time. Christine holds Kererū while he is being anaesthetised.

3 Kererū in his cage after surgery. The fixator holds the pins in place.

4 Daily weigh-in.

5 New feathers growing back around the pins.

6 Kererū looking good and nearly ready to go.

7 Kererū kai: fruit, seeds and vegetables.

8 A broken wing *and* a broken bill. This kererū should have been more careful!

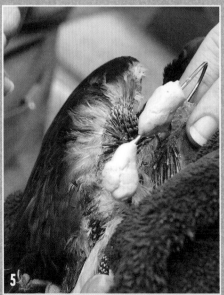

HOW TO CARE FOR KERERŪ

Whoosh, whoosh. It's spring! Kererū is on top of the world. He's invincible! He's Superbird! He soars over houses, turns and twists, angles between high trees, zooms up a driveway, flips over a fence, heads for the bush behind town.

Cat is dreaming in the armchair. Whiskers twitch, paws flick.

Whoosh! Smash! Bonk!

A heavy object thuds into the plate glass window.

Cat knows what this means! She's out the door faster than you can say *jellymeat*.

But the children in the house also know, and are out the door quicker than you can say *cat*.

By the time they arrive, cat has a mouth full of Kererū and is working out what to do next. She's never had such a fabulous catch.

'Kitty, kitty, good cat.' They stroke her head, lever her jaws apart and carefully take Kererū indoors. He is stunned, his bill is bloody, his wing dangles. Mum wraps him in a towel and puts him in a box. 'It's off to the vet for *you*,' she says.

Kererū are a common native species and regularly seen in bushier parts of New Zealand towns and forests, but their carefree, swooping flight means there's often at least one in the Wildbase wards.

Birds often crash into windows. The glass reflects the sky and the trees and sometimes they can see through, so the windows are not visible to them. If you flew into a window at speed it would feel as if the air had abruptly turned to stone. Many die.

This bird has trauma to its head and bill. Its keel (breastbone) is fractured and its wing is broken. Three days after it comes in, its wing is pinned and held in place by a fixator, like a little bridge that prevents movement while it is healing.

And then it's a matter of eating and sleeping, waiting and mending. New feathers grow. Once the bandages come off and the pins come out, Kererū is off to the Turakina Bird Rescue centre for more rest and recuperation before he is sent home and back up into that blue, blue sky.

Whoosh, whoosh.

Mind how you go, Kererū. ★

CASE # 78562

KERERŪ / WOOD PIGEON
Hemiphaga novaeseelandiae

Conservation status: Not threatened.
Admitted: 01/03/17
Injury: Fractured wing.

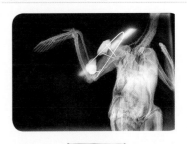

Kererū are vital for forest health because they are the only species able to swallow and spread the large seeds of trees such as pūriri, taraire and kohekohe. We'd be sunk without them!

HOW TO TEND TAKAHĒ

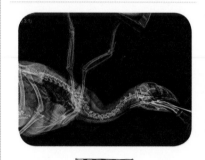
When the patient on the operating table is one of only perhaps 300 birds of a particular species alive *in the whole world*, that's a Big Deal! The takahē named Mere came from an island off the coast of Rakiura/Stewart Island when she was three. She was moved to the Burwood Takahē Centre, not far from Te Anau, and while she was there, the recovery team saw a small lump on her cloaca.*

The lump grew, so Mere was flown to Wildbase. She was stressed and her heart was beating *way too fast*. She was put in isolation, fed with specially enriched food called Harrison's Recovery Mix and left overnight to calm down.

X-rays and tests the next day showed a soft pulpy cyst, like a big round blister. There was no other infection and no obvious cause.

The liquid was drawn out of the cyst but it came back in a couple of days, so six days after Mere was admitted, she was operated on and the cyst was removed.

Everything was sweet. She lost blood in the incubator after surgery, but was stable when she returned to her room. The team put barrier cream on the wound to keep it clean and fed her with extra-grunty food.

Two weeks later she was great. The scar healed nicely and although her weight was lower, she was eating well. She was sent to Ngā Manu Nature Reserve in Waikanae for four weeks and then sent to nearby Mana Island to join its small takahē population.

Sadly, Mere was found dead only one month later. Fluid had leaked from her intestine, causing infection and death. It was a great shame because she had been doing so well.

Takahē are distantly related to pūkeko but are larger, more brightly coloured and cannot fly. In the wild, they eat tussock, tussock seeds and fern roots.

Takahē were seen only four times in the 1800s and then not at all. For many years people thought they were extinct, but a small population was discovered in Fiordland's remote Murchison Mountains in 1948. (The North Island takahē, the moho, *has* gone forever.)

There are still wild takahē in the Murchison Mountains but mostly today they are in safe places such as Ngā Manu or Mana Island. There are just over 300 takahē left *in the world*, twice as many as in 1981 — but still so precarious.

1

1 This takahē was in Wildbase in 2014 for repair of a damaged bill.

2 Takahē Mere, out cold before surgery.

3 The troublesome cyst.

4 Takahē Maroro, another takahē, being weighed.

5, 6 & 7 Birds can develop a condition called bumblefoot, especially when they walk on hard surfaces a lot. Bumblefoot causes swelling and thickening of the toes and feet. Takahē Maroro was treated for it twice and the second time some of her middle toe was amputated.

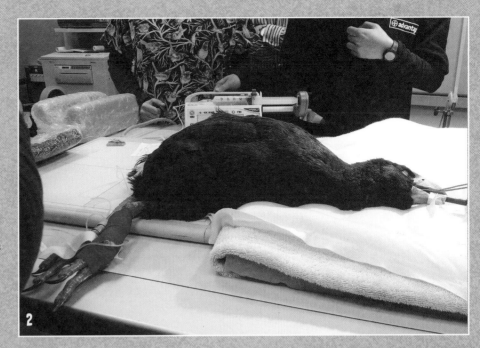

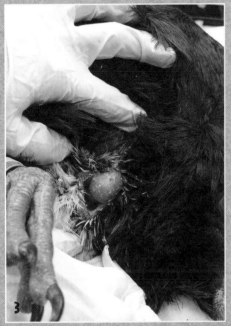

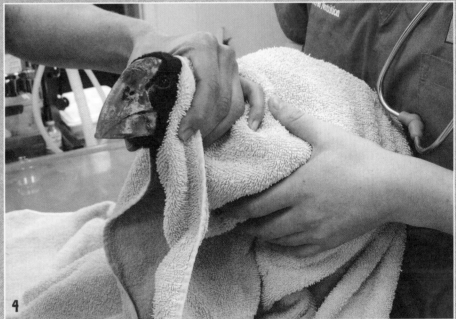

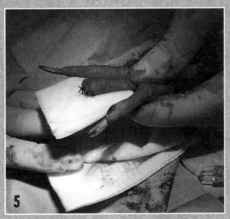

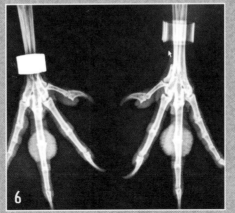

1 Kākā in her cage in late March 2017, while she was waiting to hear whether she would be going to Pukaha Mount Bruce.

2 & 4 This curious kākā was admitted to Wildbase in May 2012 suffering from starvation and exhaustion.

3 The 2012 kākā is X-rayed. Note the spectacular under-wing colour.

5 Kākā kai — just like Kea's. Heaps of fruit and vegetables, with seeds in the bottom for afters.

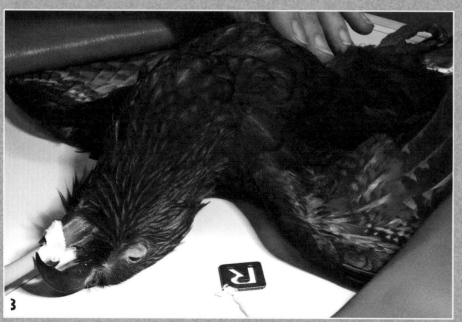

HOW TO FATTEN KĀKĀ

Sometimes things go wrong, even in the best of places. Kāpiti Island, over the Rauoterangi Channel opposite the busy, buzzing towns of Paraparaumu and Waikanae, is a wildlife paradise for New Zealand species including the bush parrot or kākā. Ancient and regenerating trees are full of hidey-holes and nesting sites and there are plenty of seeds, fruit, nectar, sap and invertebrates to eat. It's a wildlife sanctuary so it's safe from predators like rats, stoats, cats and possums.

Kākā are loving it . . . *with one exception!*

In early March 2017, a young female kākā was found alone and scavenging in a rubbish trailer on a Paraparaumu street. She was listless, seriously underweight and easily captured when an apple was waved under her bill. She was quite friendly. She was taken to Ngā Manu Nature Reserve and sent on to Wildbase.

What was the problem?

On day 1, when she was examined, she was so badly dehydrated the team was unable to take blood. But she was given fluids and liquid food and was also hungry enough to eat by herself.

Tests over the following week drew a blank. Nothing was broken! There were no parasites! She wasn't poisoned!

She was just very thin and malnourished.

In the end the team speculated that she flew or was blown from the island to the mainland and simply didn't know how to go home or look after herself.

Over the remainder of March and early April, Kākā was given heaps of nutritious food, both whole food in her bowl as well as liquid food in a tube down her gullet.

Every few days, she was heavier.

Just look at her progress: 9 March = 290 grams; 13 March = 390 grams; 21 March = 438 grams; 26 March = 468 grams; 3 April = 480grams; 17 April = 518 grams.

If she had continued at that rate, she would soon have been unable to fly!

Her food was cut back a little and she was moved to the large display room at Wildbase where she had space to exercise and build up her muscles.

Towards the end of April she went to Pukaha Mount Bruce Wildlife Centre on the other side of the Tararua Ranges. *Not far from Kāpiti as the kākā flies!*

If all goes according to plan, she will eventually be released at Boundary Stream in Hawke's Bay.

CASE # 79313

KĀKĀ / BUSH PARROT
Nestor meridionalis

Conservation status: Nationally vulnerable.

Admitted: 09/03/2017

Condition: Thin; apparently starving.

Kākā are found on all three main islands of New Zealand as well as a number of offshore islands. They are forest dwellers and are not often seen above the timber line, although a number have become city kids in Wellington after overflowing from Zealandia, the city's wildlife sanctuary. They are smaller than kea and more olive-brown in colour.

5

HOW TO HEAL HOIHO

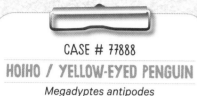

CASE # 77888

HOIHO / YELLOW-EYED PENGUIN

Megadyptes antipodes

Conservation status: Nationally endangered.

Admitted: 10/12/2016

Injury: Slash wounds on both feet.

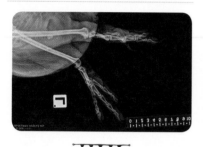

* This penguin could be a male or a female. No one knows because they are so similar: take your pick!

1

Hoiho #77888 is hot and stressed from the long journey north when she* is admitted to Wildbase on 10 December 2016. She was picked up at Long Point on the south coast of the South Island two days earlier. She has slash wounds on both feet. A long, slow process begins.

There are several operations to clean the wounds and she's given an ongoing cocktail of drugs to relieve pain and treat infection. Her right hock is kept bandaged and gradually improves over the first month. Hoiho has a good appetite and enjoys eating salmon, anchovies and fish fillets. She's given a vitamin supplement because her fish has been frozen, and freezing destroys some of its goodness.

In mid-January Hoiho catches her toe in rubber matting in her room and tears a claw: it's a minor setback but a larger problem looms. When her bandage is removed on 20 January, it seems at first that all is well. The wound is closed and healing. In the morning she's OK but by afternoon her left leg is wobbly and unstable. *Oh no.* As well as the cuts that are healing there is damage to tendons, the tissues that connect muscle to bone and hold legs straight.

Another round of X-rays and investigation follows and a new plan is hatched. Hoiho's leg is put into a thermoplastic splint that can be moulded to her own special foot shape. More time passes.

A month later Hoiho is so much better that she stands most of the time instead of sitting back on her hocks. By 24 February she has her first swim in the pool at the large-animal treatment unit, and three days later she is in the water for six and a half hours, no problem. Sweet. On 2 March she is flown south. She is released at Long Point the next day. She has been at Wildbase for 83 days.

Long Point is a lonely finger of land on the south coast of Otago. Hoiho come ashore every evening and climb to their homes in the hills. Each day they go to sea. They dive as deep as 120 metres in search of small and medium-sized fish to eat.

But something has changed in recent years in that watery world beyond the rocky coves, shingle beaches and crashing white surf of the Canterbury and Otago coastline, a vicious *something* that slashes the feet, hocks and tummies of hoiho. So many are being found with these injuries that a dedicated Hoiho Hospital has been set up in Otago for six weeks each year, just to care for them.

Some suspect the penguins are being attacked by barracouta, a savage hungry fish with pointy fangs, but there are many possible causes, including sharks biting them. W*hat's going on?*

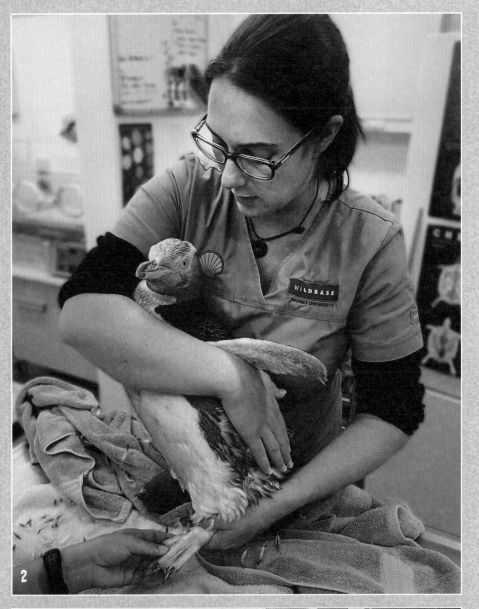

1 Hoiho eat small and medium fish — and could be getting in the way of barracouta when they are hunting the same prey. Or is something else causing these nasty wounds?

2 Pauline holds a hoiho while it is being examined.

3 Hoiho doesn't put up with any nonsense. She holds her ground in her room at the hospital, back to the corner, head up and challenging, eyes watchful, ready to whack anyone who comes near. And that bill delivers a painful bite!

4 Out cold for X-ray and work-up. You can see the rip on this hoiho's leg.

5 Let's see what you weigh today.

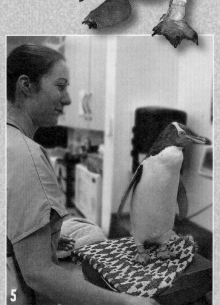

1 Tuatara can lift his head — but that's about it.

2 *What is it, Tuatara? What's wrong?*

3 The daily soak in water to help rehydrate him.

4 A tiny green gecko looking a bit like Kermit.

HOW TO TREAT TUATARA

When he arrives at Wildbase on 21 March 2017 Tuatara is as floppy as an empty sock. His legs are paralysed and he isn't moving his tail. He can slightly move his head. There are no obvious signs of what is wrong.

Tuatara is a male aged 11 years, young for this species. He is not tame but has lived all his life in a wildlife park in an enclosure with a number of other reptiles.

Many tests are carried out during Tuatara's first week at Wildbase. His blood is analysed and X-rays and a CT scan are taken. Nothing shows aside from small signs of inflammation. Perhaps he has eaten crickets that were accidentally contaminated with insecticides?

There's not much hope for him but he is treated anyway, with antibiotics, and morphine for pain relief. He is put in water to soak each day because he is so dehydrated and can absorb the moisture through his skin.

For the first week there is no change.

On 27 March, however, a number of people think that maybe, just *maybe*, they see Tuatara's left leg move when he is being treated. *Is it a trick of the light? Are they imagining things*?

Nothing moves rapidly in the tuatara world.

Day by day, in tiny, tiny amounts, Tuatara improves. He's fed about a teaspoon of fish and reptile food called 'Repashy', and on 2 April, *hey, look!* he's found with a cricket in his mouth.

OK, he can't *chew* or *swallow* it, but it's a positive sign.

By 17 April, nearly a month after admission, he's moving all limbs. He is being soaked every other day and is eating all his food. The team is very pleased when he produces a giant poo.

A week later he is enjoying a short daily bask in the sun and getting stroppy about being handled. He's ready to go home.

Tuatara are not the only reptiles treated at Wildbase, of course. New Zealand's native lizards, geckos and skinks also come to Wildbase from captive breeding programmes. Like most creatures, they can suffer from a range of conditions including nutritional disorders, parasites and fungal and bacterial infections, especially to their delicate skin.

CASE # 79491

TUATARA
Sphenodon punctatus

Conservation status: Relict (numbers low but stable; were once declining).
Admitted: 21/03/17
Condition: Paralysed.

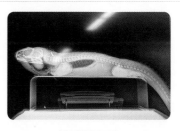

Tuatara are called 'living fossils' because this species was around at least 200 million years ago. They are the *only* surviving members of the Sphenodon family.

Tuatara are not fully grown until they are around 35 years old and they live from 60 to 100 years. New Zealand's wild tuatara are either on islands or in wildlife sanctuaries.

HOW TO DETOX WHIO

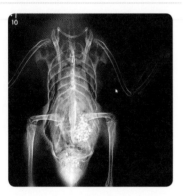
Whio was first spotted in early April 2017 by trampers Anthony Behrens and Fiona Burleigh. He was alone on a shingle bar beside the bustling Makaroro River, not far from where it flows out of the Ruahine Ranges into the farmland of Central Hawke's Bay. They could see at once he had been in the wars. His feathers were bedraggled and one wing drooped. He limped under a log and sadly whistled his breathy call: *whi-oo*.

A message was sent to conservationist Ben Douglas, who walked in and carried Whio out. He handed him over to Janet Wilson from the Ruahine Whio Protection Trust. She was going to Palmerston North and dropped Whio into Wildbase.

When Whio was assessed he was very thin, he could not stand, and his tail flick was slow. Rebecca, the vet, could tell he was an old bird. He was given fluids, liquid food and pain relief and put in an incubator in intensive care. His X-ray the next day showed nothing was broken but there were traces of lead in his blood.

Lead is a soft, heavy metal that does not rust. Humans have used it for thousands of years for a long list of things — in building, plumbing, batteries, bullets and weights. For a long time no one knew that it is terribly toxic. It damages the nervous system and causes brain damage and blood disorders.

But how did Whio get poisoned?

No one knows, but there's lead in the environment from all sorts of sources including from lead shot and lead bullets used in hunting.

And why was he by himself? Whio are usually in pairs but are very territorial. Perhaps he had been in a scrap.

Luckily, he was soon sorted. A process called *chelation* removed the lead and in just over two weeks Whio was splashing like a duckling in the clamshell pool that had been moved into the display room at the hospital. He was discharged on 12 April and released back in the hills where he was found.

Wildbase treats around 105 native birds for lead poisoning *every year*. The parrots, kākā and kea, are most likely to suffer because lead is soft and tastes sweet to them. They nibble old lead-head nails, pick at lead flashing on buildings, scavenge in dumps and help themselves to car wheel weights.

The best people can do is not encourage them so they don't become tame and so they eat where they should — in the wild.

1

1 A younger, different whio in 2014. It was thin, and had an old wing injury that was helped with surgery.

2 Whio has a catheter in his leg to deliver medication.

3 & 4 Out cold for work-up. X-ray time.

5 Whio is still battered, but brighter after one week at Wildbase.

6 Whio in his cage in the ward. He has a little box to hide in plus bowls of food. He makes a right mess at night, sploshing in the bowls.

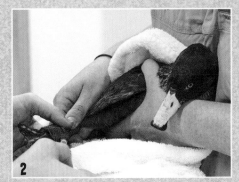

1

2

3

4

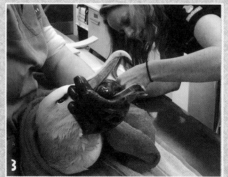

5

1 The Salvin's mollymawk revving up for release.

2 Can you see him? He's in the exercise pool in the large animal treatment unit at the vet school.

3 A catheter is being inserted into Shy mollymawk's leg. Note the thick gloves!

4 This is a Sooty albatross being X-rayed.

5 *Away, away!* The Shy mollymawk is back on salt water and off out to sea.

HOW TO MEDICATE MOLLYMAWK

2013 was a year of extreme weather. A long dry summer was wiped out by massive storms in winter, with pelting rain, tearing winds and giant ocean waves. Most birds that are hurt or die at sea just disappear beneath the surface of the blue-grey briny, but a few end up on shore or further inland.

In early December two large seabirds turned up at Wildbase within a week. The first, a rare Salvin's mollymawk, was found on a farm near Levin. It didn't seem hurt but it couldn't take off. It was caught and even taken to school for *show and tell* before it was handed to the Department of Conservation and driven to Wildbase.

When it was assessed, it had signs of old (healed) injuries but its main problem was blindness in its right eye. An eye vet examined it and found a clouded lens (a cataract). But mollymawks can manage with one eye, so it was given TLC for 10 days and released at sea near Levin.

The second bird, a Shy mollymawk (that's its name), was a more complex case. It was found not far away on Foxton beach. It was tired, floppy and anaemic (had low iron levels). There was also a puzzling redness between its toes, but nothing was broken and at first everything else seemed normal.

However, over the next days it became clear that something was seriously amiss in its lungs. When it breathed, it made wet, gurgling sounds, and one morning it coughed up mucous. It often regurgitated its food, and one time it sat in it afterwards, making a right mess of itself and its enclosure.

It was treated for bacterial and fungal infection and for worms. It was given iron and vitamins. It was tube-fed fish slurry as well as fresh fish.

It slowly gained weight, from 2238 grams to 3001 grams. That's a lot for a small creature.

By 17 December it was standing and looking around but it had bumblefoot or pododermatitis (pressure sores on its feet) and its right wing was drooping. Nevertheless, it was taken to the vet school's large animal unit for a wash and a swim. It preened and stretched its wings. Each day it swam for longer, up to five hours. Its droopy wing was getting stronger. Things were looking up!

The Shy mollymawk was released at sea off the Foxton coast on 23 December. It sat on the water for a few minutes then flew 50 metres.

Yeay!

CASES # 62499 & 62409

1] Salvin's mollymawk/
Thalassarche salvini
Conservation status: Nationally critical.
Admitted: 10/12/13
Condition: Grounded.

2] Shy mollymawk/
Thalassarche cauta
Conservation status: Declining.
Admitted: 02/12/13
Condition: Lethargic.

Mollymawks are medium-sized albatrosses. They are the most common albatrosses in the Southern Hemisphere.

New Zealand is the seabird capital of the world! Around 80 seabird species breed here, and many of those are endemic, which means they breed nowhere else.

HOW TO REVITALISE BITTERN

CASE # 79577

AUSTRALASIAN BITTERN / MATUKU HŪREPO

Botaurus poiciloptilus

Conservation status: Nationally endangered.

Admitted: 25/03/14

Condition: Emaciated (very thin).

Bitterns are large heron-sized birds. Males can weigh 1400 grams, females 900 grams.

* Humans might *hear* rather than *see* bitterns. In the breeding season, males make deep booming calls across the wetland to attract females.

1

The wetland is a soft, soggy place, full of pools, light, mud and reeds. It's the home of tuna/eels, frogs, koura/freshwater crayfish and trillions of water-loving insects as well as the birds that eat them, including bittern.

Few humans have ever seen this bird because it is a camouflage supremo.* Not only does its stippled tan and brown plumage blend perfectly into the wetland background, but it is also ultra-shy. It lies low in daylight and feeds in the early morning, the evening and at night, and when danger comes near, it tilts its long bill to the sky and sways back and forth just like a reed. (Astonishing fact: it can see around both sides of its own neck!)

The bittern admitted to Wildbase in March 2014 was found in a paddock on a farm near Taupō. Its age and gender were unknown. It was so thin and weak it could not stand. It weighed 848.9 grams.

Sally, the Taupō vet, could find nothing obviously wrong and sent the bird to Dawne at the Turakina Bird Rescue Centre. She in turn bumped it along to Wildbase. X-rays and blood tests also showed nothing but it was clearly unwell.

Why was it ill?

What had happened to it?

As in so many cases, we can only guess.

The bittern was given fluids and was force-fed fish slurry as well as liquid food for insect-eating birds. It was also given pieces of chicken and fish.

Over the next two weeks it came right. It ate by itself and it gained weight until it weighed 1122 grams. It was driven to Bird Rescue at Turakina on 9 April and later returned to its wetland. It seems it just needed a little holiday.

Australasian bitterns are disappearing under our noses! They are found in New Zealand, Australia and New Caledonia but are now so rare in all three countries that they are ranked as globally endangered. Their furtive ways make them hard to count but it is thought that there are fewer than 900 in New Zealand.

The main cause is the loss of their wetland homes — the place where they eat, are relatively safe and can breed.

But they are also attacked and killed by by cats, rats, dogs, stoats, ferrets and weasels and sometimes they are hit by cars or fly into power lines.

And sometimes things just happen that we will never know about.

1 A bittern fluffing its feathers out so it looks
  larger. Bitterns are so shy that they really
  hate being in hospital!

2 *If I hold my head up, I'll be invisible!*
  Even though it's in an enclosure, this
  bittern is doing the only thing it knows to
  keep safe — pretending to be a reed.

3 A broken wing.

4 A bittern under general anaesthetic.
  Look at its excellent fish-stabbing bill.

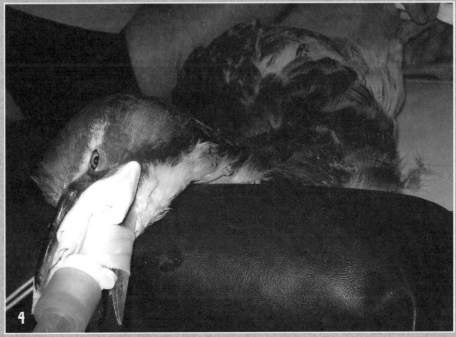

1 The Taranaki falcon in the incubator with both legs bandaged.

2 A falcon with a broken wing in 2016. The blobs that look like plasticine are part of a fixator like the one used on the kererū on page 39. They are made from fast-setting epoxy putty called 'Knead-it' from the hardware store. They help hold the pins in place. The pink bandage is holding his wing, and his tail feathers — so important for flying — are wrapped in plastic to prevent damage.

3 Another raptor, a harrier hawk, at Wildbase in March 2017. This bird was hit by a car while it was feeding on the road and had a broken wing.

4 & 5 Morepork, from Levin, in June 2016. He was pulled out of the grille of a truck, lucky to be alive. He looks as if he is wondering how to eat his chicken dinner with a bandaged foot. Morepork on the day of his release.

6 Harrier hawk feathers, plucked from its leg before its operation.

HOW TO FIX FALCON

Falcon is a true Sky Lord. He's not only tremendously agile but is able to fly at speeds of up to 100 kilometres an hour. Hard luck if you are a small bird and Falcon fancies a snack . . . you can twist and turn and flutter but you will be out-flown and out-manoeuvred, seized by sharp talons and killed with one bite.

Like Kererū on page 38, the male falcon admitted to Wildbase in February 2016 is knocked out cold when he flies full-tilt into a farm window. He is found by the family fox terrier, rescued, taken to the vet in New Plymouth and sent to Wildbase.

X-rays next morning show that the right femur — the big bone at the top of the leg — is fractured. Falcon is taken directly to surgery. The break is pinned and attached to an external skeletal fixator. He is given pain relief, antibiotics and anti-inflammatory medicines.

A week later, the wound is good but his right wing is drooping; he is getting poo on his feathers so the wing is bandaged to protect it and keep it still.

He's on a diet of dead one-day-old chicks and slowly gaining weight.

It seems Falcon is mending, but by 20 March all is not well. There is a persistent leaky discharge around one of the pins; on 21 March, Falcon is sitting on his hocks and he wobbles when he tries to stand.

On further investigation, it seems he has a folding fracture in his *left* tibiotarsus, his shin bone. The leg is swollen and sore but doesn't need to be pinned. Instead a modified splint bandage holds it in place.

Calcium and vitamin D powder are added to his diet to help healing.

But then, to complicate matters, the break in his right leg is not quite right. It must be *perfect* for a bird that depends on accuracy to survive, so it's back to the operating table for Falcon.

At last, things start to improve.

By 5 May, Falcon is perching well and eating two chicks a day. Being a wild, independent creature, he is easily stressed so handling is kept to a minimum — his meds are even hidden in his food.

A week later he is well enough to be moved to the aviary in the veterinary school's large animal unit. He flies around and is very interested in the starlings outside — a great sign, although not so promising for the starlings.

He returns to his home in the Taranaki countryside on 26 May.

Look out, little birds!

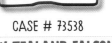

CASE # 73538

NEW ZEALAND FALCON / KĀREAREA

Falco novaeseelandiae

Conservation status: Nationally vulnerable.

Admitted: 24/2/2016

Injury: Broken legs.

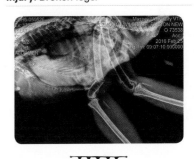

Falcons/kārearea, harriers/kāhu and morepork/ruru are New Zealand's best-known raptors or birds of prey. Raptors hunt for their food.

6

CASE HISTORY SNAPSHOTS

As many as 50 different species come to Wildbase every year, some from as far away as the subantarctic islands and the Chathams Islands. They include:

OCEAN-FLIERS such as albatross, petrel, shearwater, gannet, penguin, prion

SHORE-HUGGERS such as dotterel, gull, heron, shag

WATER & WETLAND LOVERS such as duck, kingfisher, swan, pūkeko

BUSH BABIES such as kākāpō, kākāriki, robin, long-tailed cuckoo, shining cuckoo, weka and the honey-eaters, kōkako, tūī, bellbird, waxeye

Some, like weka, heron and kingfisher, are found across a range of environments.

WEKA • 07/14
Leg injury

PIED SHAG / KĀRUHIRUHI • 03/16
Tangled in a fishing line

KŌKAKO • 11/14
Dermatitis

KĀKĀPŌ • 09/04
Leg fracture

KINGFISHER / KŌTARE • 09/11
Hit window, run over by skateboard

DABCHICK / WEWEIA • 03/13
Weak, emaciated

PŪKEKO / SWAMP HEN • 06/13
Hit by a vehicle

TŪĪ • 07/14
Flew into a window

WAXEYE / TAUHOU • 08/11
Wing fracture

KĀKĀRIKI / RED-CROWNED PARAKEET • 01/14
Pneumonia

ROYAL SPOONBILL / KŌTUKU NGUTUPAPA • 05/13
Weak, emaciated

WHITE-FACED HERON / MATUKU • 07/16
Wing fracture

NORTHLAND GREEN GECKO • 06/14
Fungal dermatitis

COOK'S PETREL / TĪTĪ • 10/14
Wing fracture

ERECT-CRESTED PENGUIN • 04/15
Parasitism, and getting ready to moult

SHORT-TAILED BAT / PEKAPEKA • 03/09
Ear dermatitis

RED-BILLED GULL / TARĀPUNGA • 06/16
Swallowed a fishing line

SHEARWATER / TĪTĪ • 05/16
Wrecked in a storm

GANNET / TĀKAPU (JUV) • 03/12
Found lost on a ski slope 260 km away

BLACK PETREL / TĀIKO • 07/12
Both feet hurt

HUTTON'S SHEARWATER • 04/15
Injured in a storm at sea

And then, of course, there's a small crew of other creatures. Some are paying customers, such as Tina the tortoise. She lives at the Feilding Childcare Centre and has been a regular at Wildbase since her foot was bitten by another tortoise.

Or Cadbury, the loveable galah, who came to have his wing repaired and had to be given a collar so he wouldn't pick his bandages apart — another parrot family creature like Kea! The air was blue with shrieks and curses when he was being treated. Everyone loved him.

GREEN TURTLE / HONU • 11/14
Fungal pneumonia

CADBURY THE GALAH • 03/17
Injured wing

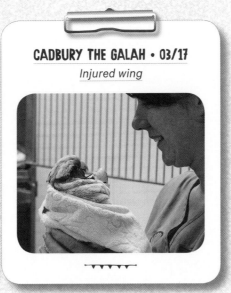

RED PANDA • 03/14
Dental disease

TINA THE TORTOISE • 07/14
Tortoise bite

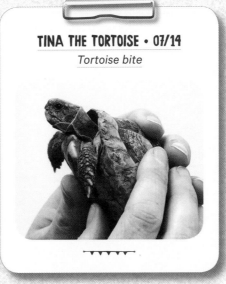

MUSCOVY DUCK • 03/17
Dog attack victim

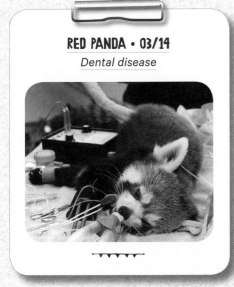

HOW TO PUT WILDBASE OUT OF BUSINESS!

What if . . . there were no moreporks hanging out of truck grilles, no birds crashing into windows, no kiwi or penguins bitten by dogs, no bitterns high and dry without wetlands?

So many of the animals that arrive at vet clinics and at Wildbase have needless injuries. We could all do little things to help our native animals, such as . . .

WATCH THOSE CARS! Car and truck strikes kill and maim huge numbers of birds, especially in spring and early summer when fledglings are still getting the hang of flying. Eyes wide! Take care out there!

COLLAR THAT CAT! Bells, bibs and bright cat collars make it easier for birds to know the cat is about. *Curfew* that cat from the moment it's a kitten! Early morning and evening are favourite times to hunt.

DITCH THE DOG! Keep it on a lead or leave it at home when you are around wildlife. Please don't let dogs disturb birds on beaches because that's the only space for them to feed and nest in. Flightless birds such as little blue penguins and kiwi are so easily hurt and killed.

HANDS IN POCKETS! If you see what looks like an injured bird, wait a sec in case it's a fledgling that is being fed and cared for on the ground by its parents. Only pick it up if you are really, *really* sure it needs help.

STICKER THOSE WINDOWS! It's crazy to think our buildings are killing birds. Put special window alert stickers on the glass: *we* can hardly see them but they glow like stop lights for birds.

LOCK UP THE LEAD! Don't spray lead ammunition into the environment. It's deadly for everyone — you and me included.

BAG THE PLASTIC! Keep all that choking, snaring plastic out of waterways and oceans. Plastic tops, plastic nets, plastic bags . . . they have no place in the sea or inside marine wildlife.

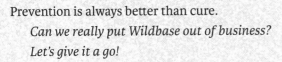

Prevention is always better than cure.

Can we really put Wildbase out of business?

Let's give it a go!

HUIA
LAST SEEN: 1907

HOW TO READ THREAT LEVELS

The New Zealand Threat Classification System is a carefully developed scale that tells us what shape our native animals are in. Scientists consider several different criteria when they assess the health of a species and are constantly reviewing and updating the lists. They ask:

1   **POPULATION SIZE** How many breeding adults are there? How large is the place where they live?

2   **POPULATION TREND** Is the population going *up* or *down*? How rapidly is this happening?

STEPHENS ISLAND WREN
LAST SEEN: 1894

There are two categories, each with sub-sections.

THREATENED = In serious trouble and in great danger of dying out.

A   **NATIONALLY CRITICAL** Nationally critical species are at *immediate* risk of dying out.

B   **NATIONALLY ENDANGERED** } These mean serious trouble as well, but a

C   **NATIONALLY VULNERABLE** } teeny bit less than 'nationally critical'.

AT RISK = Not immediately likely to die out, but if their numbers continue to fall or a new threat arises, that could easily change. They are in some trouble.

A   **DECLINING** Numbers falling, but still common

B   **RECOVERING** Numbers low but increasing after previously declining

C   **RELICT** Low numbers but stable after previously declining

D   **NATURALLY UNCOMMON** A naturally small population that could easily become more endangered

Read more online at http://www.doc.govt.nz/nature/conservation-status/

INDEX

ILLUSTRATIONS

Images copyright © as below, 2017
Key: b = bottom; t = top; m = middle; l = left; r = right
Dave Wiltshire: p.5; p.6 bl; p.7 tr; p.8 b; p.21 b; p.31 t; p.33 t; p.42 tr, br; p.47 br;
p.56 br; p.57 tl, tm, br; p.58 tr; p.59 tl, bl.
Anja Kohler: p.24; p.25 t, br; p.26. Nigel Dougherty: p.13; p.25 bl.
Maritime NZ: p.28 b; p.29 tl, tr, b; p.30 (all); p.32 bl, br; p.33 br.
All others are either by Wildbase Hospital or the author.

THANKS

The author's name appears on the cover but she does not write in isolation.
I'm grateful to the following for their generous contributions, unstinting assistance and encouragement:
Nicola Legat, Anna Bowbyes, Pauline Nijman, Brett Gartrell, Dawne Morton,
Dawn Mills, Barbara Larson, Tessa Lyons, Dave Wiltshire, Nigel Dougherty, Kate Hebblethwaite,
Philip Marsh, Jasmine Pavey, Rebekah Cullen, Eva Laing, Christine Tan, Carina Svensson, Rebecca Webster,
Janet Wilson, Anthony Behrens, Fiona Burleigh and Ben Douglas.
As always, thanks to Peter Haines and my family, friends, neighbours and co-conservationists.
You know who you are!

MASSEY UNIVERSITY PRESS

First published in 2017 by Massey University Press
Private Bag 102904, North Shore Mail Centre, Auckland 0745, New Zealand
www.masseypress.ac.nz

Text copyright © Janet Hunt, 2017
Design by Janet Hunt

The moral right of the author has been asserted

A catalogue record for this book is available from the National Library of New Zealand

Printed and bound in China by 1010 Printing International Ltd
ISBN: 978-0-9941407-1-5